Sometimes we find ourselves in a situation we would much prefer not to be in. Whatever the cause of your suffering and sadness, the heart aches and God hears the heart's cry.

This little book is full of words to comfort and refresh you, and work in you their healing. Let this time of pain become a place of transforming, a place where you can lean back into God's love and feel the understanding and support.

Come to me all
who are heavily laden
and I will refresh you.
Matthew 11:28

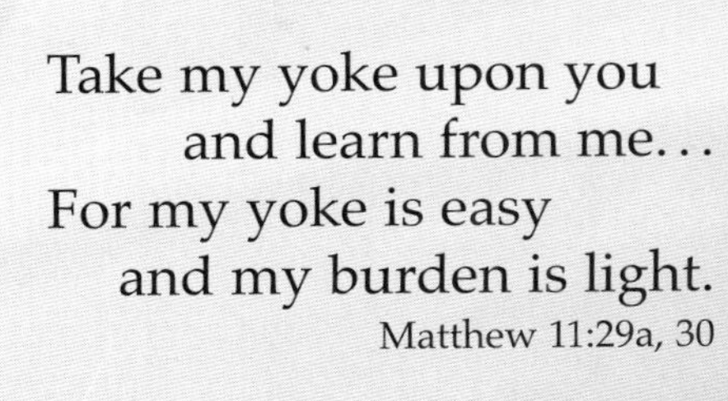

Take my yoke upon you
and learn from me…
For my yoke is easy
and my burden is light.
Matthew 11:29a, 30

Don't be afraid.
I am with you always.

Hide me
in the shadow
of your wings.
Psalm 17:8b

Your love surrounds me
and will not let me go.

My soul clings to you;
your right hand holds me fast.
Psalm 36:8

Though I walk through the valley
of the shadow of death
I will fear no evil.
For you are with me;
your rod and your staff
give me comfort.

Psalm 23:4

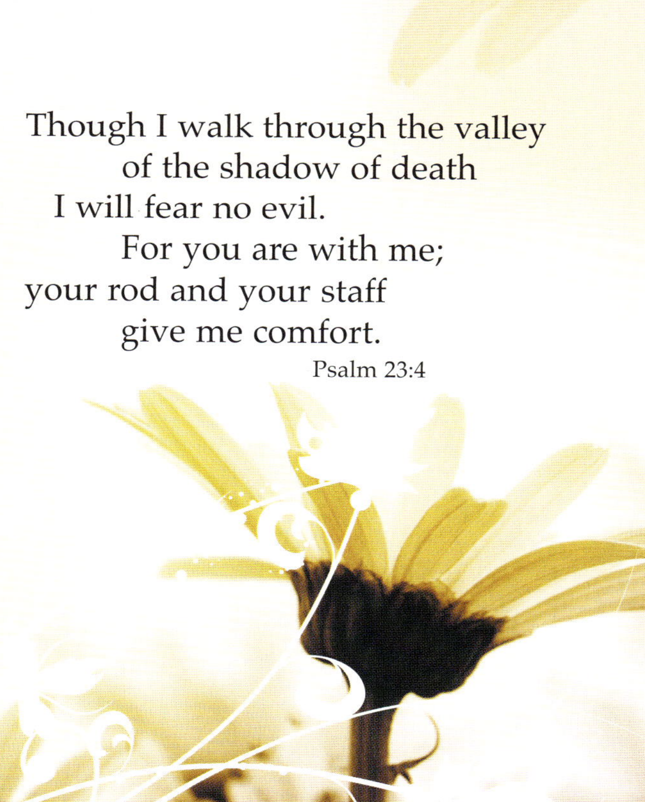

Place your hand
into the hand
of God.

God hears the cry of our hearts
and feels with us in our pain.

Let God use and transform
your suffering,
so that some good
is harvested from it.

Whisper your pain and sadness
into the listening ear of God
and let God's compassion
and comfort enfold you.

Grieving for loved ones
can never be rushed or avoided.
It is precious
and all part of our love.

Notice the bright flowers
of blessings
even in the very darkest of places.

We cannot understand
the whole picture yet.
One day we will
understand it better.

Sometimes God transforms a situation by transforming our perceptions of it.

I am convinced that neither death
nor life,
nor angels,
nor rulers,
nor things present,
nor things to come,
nor powers,
nor height,
nor depth,
nor anything else
in all creation
will be able to separate us
from the love of God
in Christ Jesus our Lord.

Romans 8:38, 39

Help us to accept the things
we cannot change,
the courage to change
the things we can
and the wisdom to know
the difference.

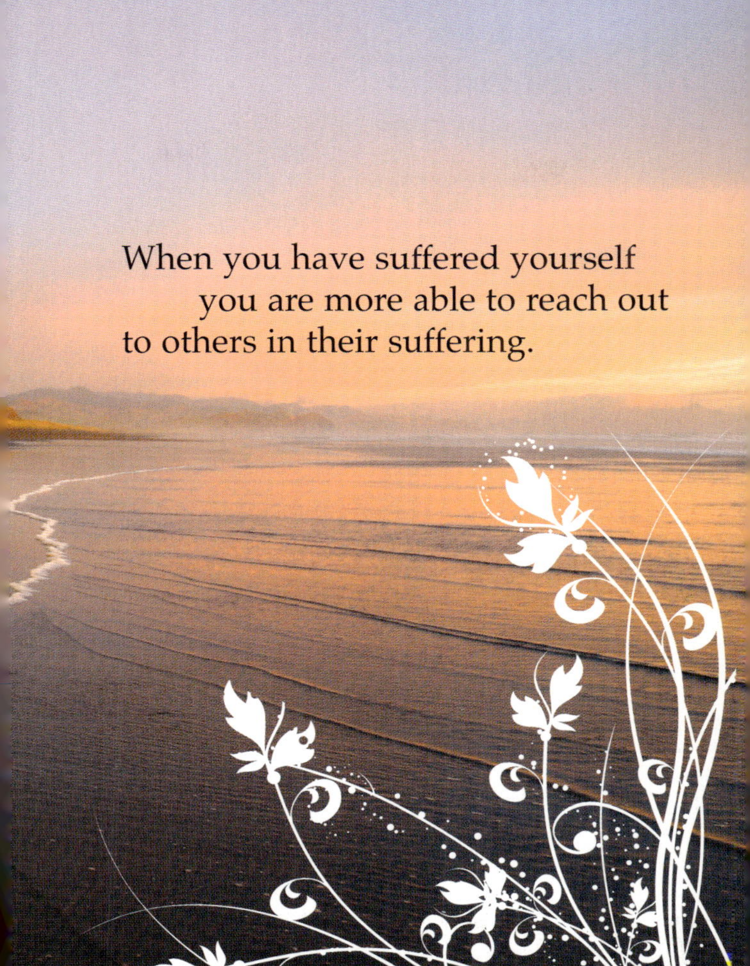

When you have suffered yourself
you are more able to reach out
to others in their suffering.

When we can
no longer walk,
God carries us.

When we get ourselves lost
the Good Shepherd is out
searching for us
and hears our bleating.

And when he finds us
he lifts us on his shoulders
and brings us safely home.

Sometimes we have no energy
or health to pray,
but that is when we are upheld
by the love
and prayers of others.

If everything feels tightly
knotted and tangled,
stop tugging at it
and allow God
to work on it.

There is nothing you can do
that would stop God loving you.
You are always his precious child.

Be gentle with yourself.

As the deer longs
for streams of water,
so longs my soul for you,
O God.

Psalm 42:1

It is only in the dark
that we can see the starlit sky.

Let God's peace melt all your
fears away.
Let his courage strengthen you.
Let his love surround you.

May God touch your pain
with healing,
and restore you to wholeness
of body, mind and spirit.

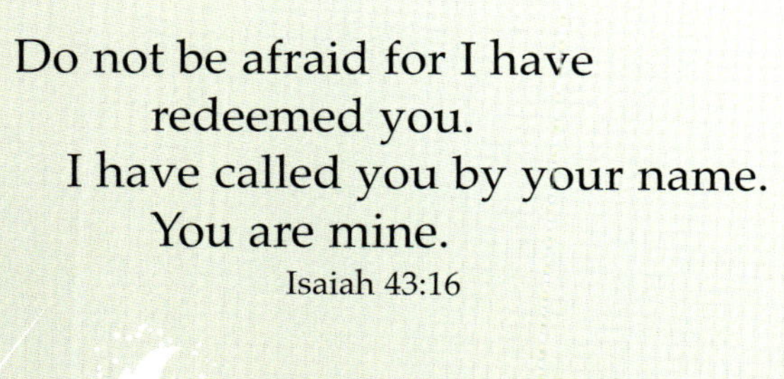

Do not be afraid for I have
redeemed you.
I have called you by your name.
You are mine.

Isaiah 43:16

God bless you
and fill you with hope,
wash your wounds
and bind them up,

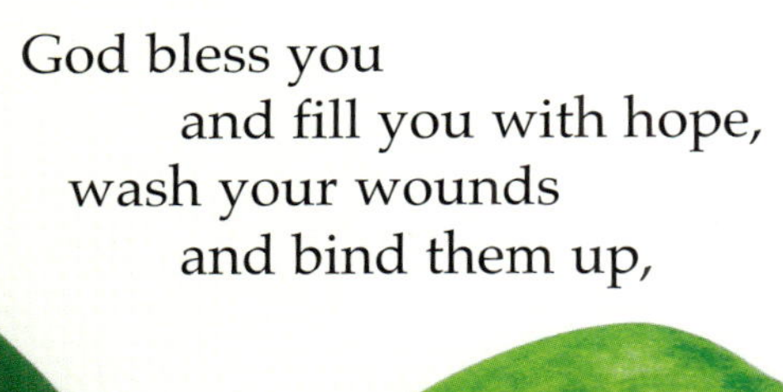

so that
you may
know the
fullness
of healing –
physical,
emotional
and
spiritual.

First published in 2007 by

KEVIN MAYHEW LTD
Buxhall, Stowmarket, Suffolk, IP14 3BW
E-mail: info@kevinmayhewltd.com
Website: www.kevinmayhew.com

Acknowledgements: The scripture quotation on page 3 was taken from the Holy Bible, New International Version. Copyright © 1973, 1978, 1984 by International Bible Society. Used by permission of Hodder and Stoughton, a member of the Hodder Headline Group. All rights reserved. NIV is a trademark of International Bible Society.

9 8 7 6 5 4 3 2 1 0

ISBN 978 1 84417 800 1
Catalogue No. 1501027

Design by Sara-Jane Came
Edited by Katherine Laidler

Printed and bound in EU